C++

The Ultimate
Beginner's Guide!

Andrew Johansen

Table of Contents

Introduction

I want to thank you and congratulate you for getting my book...

"C++: The Ultimate Beginner's Guide!"

This eBook is written for people who want to learn the basics of the C++ programming language. If you are looking for a comprehensive book that will teach you everything you need to know about C++, this just might be what you're looking for.

By reading this eBook, you'll learn the basics of C++. You'll discover the ideas, concepts, techniques, and methods used by expert C++ programmers. For example, this book will discuss variables, strings, functions, and data structures. That means you'll be able to write programs using the C++ language after reading this material.

Thanks again for purchasing this book, I hope you enjoy it!

CHAPTER 1

The C++ Programming Language – An Overview

C++ is a compiled, free-form, case-sensitive, multi-purpose, and statically typed programming language. It supports generic, procedural, and object-oriented programming.

Computer programmers consider C++ as an intermediate-level language, since it has both low-level and high-level features.

Bjarne Stroustrup, a Danish computer scientist, created C++ in 1979. Since he created this programming language as an improved version of "C" (another computer language), he called it "C with Classes." However, during 1983, the name was changed to C++.

Important Note: A language is considered as "statically typed" if type checking is conducted during the compilation.

C++ - An Objected-Oriented Programming Language

C++ is compatible with object-oriented programming. It also supports the four foundations of object-oriented software development:

- Inheritance

- Encapsulation

- Polymorphism

- Data Hiding

The Three Major Parts of C++

The C++ programming language is composed of three major parts:

1. Core Language – This part serves as the foundation of C++ programs. It includes literals, variables, operators, etc.

2. Standard Library – This part provides a wide range of functions that you can use to manipulate the core language.

3. Standard Template Library (also known as STL) – This provides you with a wide range of methods and techniques that you can use with C++.

Learning this Programming Language

When studying C++, you should concentrate on ideas and concepts related to writing codes.

You are, after all, trying to learn a programming language because you want to be a good programmer. You would want to be effective in terms of maintaining old programs and creating new ones.

This programming language is compatible with a wide range of programming techniques. You may use it as C, Smalltalk, Fortran, etc. Regardless of your preferred programming style, you'll surely achieve your goal of creating excellent programs and maintaining runtime efficiency.

Using this Programming Language

A lot of people all over the world are using C++. That means it is reliable and effective. Actually, C++ is one of the leading languages in the programming industry.

In general, programmers use C++ when writing device drivers and programs that require direct hardware control. Researchers and programming instructors use C++ to accomplish their tasks: this language is powerful and easy-to-use. Even beginners can master the basics of this language quickly.

According to computer experts, you are already using C++ if your computer runs on either Windows or Macintosh. This is because these operating systems were written using C++.

CHAPTER 2

The C++ Environment

You don't have to establish your own C++ environment when reading this book. This is because there are online tools that you can use to write and compile C++ codes. These tools are user-friendly and capable of giving immediate feedback. That means you'll quickly discover the mistakes in your programs. One of the most popular online programming tools is www.compileonline.com. You may access that site using your favorite browser as you read this eBook.

To help you get started, here's a basic code that you can use with www.compileonline.com:

```cpp
#include <iostream>
using namespace std;

int main()
{
    cout << "Hello World";
    return 0;
}
```

Try running this code on an online programming environment. You should immediately see the resulting program.

Setting Up a Local C++ Environment

If you still want to establish a local environment for the C++ language, your computer must have the following programs:

1. Text Editing Software – You'll use a text editor to write your C++ programs. Here are the text editors commonly used by C++ programmers: vi, vim, Brief, EMACS, and Windows Notepad.

    The text editor's name and version may change, depending on your machine's operating system. For instance, Notepad serves as the default text editor for Windows computers. Vi or vim, however, are compatible with UNIX, Linux, and Windows machines.

    The text files you'll produce using an editor are known as source files. In the C++ language, these files end with the following extensions: .c, .cp, or .cpp.

    Important Note: Make sure that your computer has a text editor before you use C++ locally. Without this kind of computer program, you won't be able to write any C++ code.

2. C++ Compiler – It is an actual compiler for the C++ programming language. You will use this software to compile source codes into executable programs.

    In general, compilers are not sensitive in terms of the file extension that you use for your source codes. If you won't specify the file extension, however, C++ compilers will assign .cpp (which is the default extension for this language).

    These days, the most popular compiler is the GNU C/C++ compiler.

How to Install the GNU C/C++ Compiler

- For UNIX/Linux computers – First, check whether your machine has GCC (GNU Compiler Collection). You can do this by accessing the computer's command line and entering this command:

```
$ g++ -v
```

If your computer has GCC, your screen should give you this kind of message:

```
Using built-in specs.
Target: i386-redhat-linux
Configured with: ../configure --prefix=/usr .......
Thread model: posix
gcc version 4.1.2 20080704 (Red Hat 4.1.2-46)
```

If your computer doesn't have GCC, you have to visit http://gcc.gnu.org/install to download and install it. The given webpage includes detailed instructions so you won't experience any difficulties.

- For Macintosh computers – The quickest and easiest way to get GCC is by downloading the Xcode programming environment from the Apple website. Just follow the detailed instructions provided there. Here's the link: http://developer.apple.com/technologies/tools.

- For Windows computers – You have to download and install a program called MinGW. To do this, visit www.mingw.org and access the website's download page. It would be best if you'll get the latest version of MinGW.

While getting MinGW, you should install these important programs: gcc-core, binutils, gcc-g++, and MinGW runtime. There are other supporting programs that you can download, depending on your situation and preferences.

You should add MinGW's bin subdirectory into the PATH environment variable. By doing so, you can activate the tools inside this subdirectory just by entering their basic names.

After completing the installation process, your computer will let you to run GNU tools such as ar, gcc, g++, dlltool, and ranlib using the command line.

CHAPTER 3

The Basic Syntax of the C++ Programming Language

For computer experts, C++ programs are collections of objects that interact with each other by invoking methods. At this point, let's discuss the basic elements of this language:

- Object – An object has different behaviors and states.

- Class – This is defined as a blueprint/template that defines the states/behaviors of an object.

- Method – Basically, this is the behavior of an object. Classes may contain various methods. A method is the part of the language where data is controlled, logic is written, and actions are performed.

- Instant Variable – Every object has a distinct collection of instant variables. The values given to the instant variables create that state/s of the object concerned.

The Program Structure in C++

Here's a basic C++ code that prints "Hello World."

```
#include <iostream>
using namespace std;

// main() is where program execution begins.

int main()
{
    cout << "Hello World"; // prints Hello World
    return 0;
}
```

Let's analyze the different parts of this code:

- C++ involves different headers, which hold useful or necessary data to the program. In the code given above, the **<iostream>** header is required.

- **using namespace std;** - This line asks the C++ compiler to utilize the namespace called std.

- The third line (i.e. **// main () is... begins.**) is the comment section of this programming language. C++ comments start with two slashes (i.e. //).

- **int main()** serves as the primary function where execution of the program starts.

- The fifth line tells the screen to display "This is my first C++ program."

- The last line (i.e. **return 0;**) ends the main() function and requires it to return "0" during the calling procedure.

Compiling and Executing C++ Programs

In this section of the book, you'll learn how to compile and execute C++ programs. Here are the steps you need to take:

1. Access your favorite text editor and write the code. At this point, you may enter the "Hello World" code given above.

2. Save the code as a C++-compatible source file. For this exercise, use the filename: "helloworld.cpp"

3. Access a command prompt and check the location where you stored the source file.

4. Type in "**g++ helloworld.cpp**" and hit the Enter key – this action will compile the code. If your code doesn't have any error, the command prompt will create an "a.out" file.

5. Then, run the program by typing "a.out"

6. Your computer will open a new window and show you the following message:

```
$ g++ hello.cpp
$ ./a.out
Hello World
```

Important Note: You have to ensure that g++ is in the appropriate path. Also, make sure that it runs in the location where you saved the source file.

Blocks and Semicolons in the C++ Language

In this language, you should use a semicolon to terminate a statement. Thus, each statement in your C++ codes should end with this character. Semicolons indicate the end of a programming entity.

For instance, here are four different C++ statements:

- a + b;

- add(a, b);

- b = a+1;

- a = b;

Blocks, on the other hand, are sets of logically related statements that are enclosed by curly braces. Here's an example:

```
{
    cout << "Hello World"; // prints Hello World
    return 0;
}
```

This programming language doesn't consider line endings as valid terminators. Thus, you don't have to worry about the placement of your statements. The following example will illustrate this concept:

a = b; b = b+1; add(a, b);

is similar to

a = b;

b = b+1;

add(a, b);

The Identifiers of C++

In this language, identifiers are names you use to identify classes, functions, modules, variables, or any user-defined object. Identifiers can start with a letter or an underscore. You may use numbers when naming identifiers, but you cannot use them as the initial character. Thus, "identifier1" is valid but "1identifier" is not.

You cannot use punctuation and special characters (e.g. commas, periods, dollar signs, ampersands) when naming identifiers. Additionally, the C++ programming language is case-sensitive. That means "SCIENCE", "Science", and "science" are three different identifiers.

The following list shows you several examples of valid identifiers:

- admin
- space_bar
- _perm
- z_000
- yourtitle23
- a
- z56a9
- GetVal

The Keywords in C++

Similar to other programming languages, C++ has a set of "reserved" keywords (i.e. words that cannot be used when naming variables, constants, and other identifiers). The table below will show you the keywords in the C++ language.

new	asm	try	for
if	int	do	this
else	enum	auto	true
bool	case	char	goto
void	long	throw	break
false	catch	union	class
short	const	using	while
private	explicit	protected	export
typedef	public	register	extern
typeid	typename	reinterpret_cast	return
unsigned	friend	signed	const_cast
virtual	continue	sizeof	static
default	inline	volatile	delete
struct	static_cast	wchar_t	switch
double	mutable	namespace	dynamic_cast
template			

The Trigraphs

In this programming language, some character sets have an alternate representation, known as trigraph sequence. Trigraphs are sequences that involve three characters where each sequence represents a character. Additionally each trigraph sequence begins with "??".

Here are the most popular trigraph sequences in this language:

Trigraph Sequence	Replacement
??-	~
??<	{
??>	}
??!	|
??(	[
??)	]
??=	#
??'	^
??/	\

Important Note: Some C++ compilers are not compatible with trigraph sequences. Additionally, since these sequences are inherently complex, beginners are advised to stay away from them.

Whitespace

C++ compilers ignore lines that hold whitespace. These lines are known as blank lines.

Whitespace is a word used in this language to describe tabs, blanks, comments, and newline characters. Basically, whitespaces allow you to divide your statements into smaller parts. In addition, they help compilers in identifying the beginning and end of code elements (e.g. int). Analyze the following examples:

int age;

The statement given above requires a whitespace character between age and int. The C++ compiler won't work properly if the statement is written without a whitespace character (i.e. **intage;**).

tree = leaves + wood;

For the second example, you don't have to place whitespace characters between tree and =, or between = and leaves. You can add whitespace characters to improve the readability of your C++ codes. However, these characters won't affect the resulting programs.

Comments in the C++ Language

A program comment is an explanatory statement that you may add to your codes. Comments can help people read your source codes. In general, programming languages support comments to improve the usability of the resulting computer programs.

This language allows you to place single- and multi-line comments in your codes. C++ compilers ignore characters that are placed in the code's comment section.

You should use /* to begin your comments and */ to terminate them. For instance:

/* This is an awesome comment */

You may also use // to start your comments. Here's an example:

```
#include <iostream>
using namespace std;

main()
{
    cout << "Hello World"; // prints Hello World

    return 0;
}
```

C++ compilers will ignore the part that says "**// prints Hello World**". The finished program will give you Hello World once it is executed.

CHAPTER 4

The Different Data Types and Variable Types in C++

Data Types

Like other programming languages, C++ supports different types of data. That means you have a wide range of options when it comes to storing information. C++ also allows you to use various variables, which are memory locations designed to keep values. Thus, "creating a variable" is synonymous with "reserving some memory space."

While writing your C++ programs, you'll need to store different data types (i.e. integer, Boolean, character, floating point, wide character, double floating point, etc.). Depending on the variable's data type, the OS (i.e. operating system) of your computer allots memory and determines what kind of data can be stored inside that memory.

The Primitive Types (Built-in)

This programming language offers a collection of user-defined and built-in data types. Here are the major categories of data types in C++:

Data Type	Keyword
Integer	int
Valueless	void
Character	char
Boolean	bool
Wide character	wchar_t
Double floating point	double
floating point	float

You can modify the data types given above using these modifiers:

- short

- long

- unsigned

- signed

The typedef Declaration

You may use **typedef** to assign a new name to an existing data type. Here is the syntax that you should use when making a **typedef** declaration:

```
typedef type newname;
```

For instance, the following statement informs the C++ compiler that head is an alternative term for character:

typedef char head;

Once you have executed that statement, the declaration below will be 100% valid and produce a character variable called letters:

head letters;

The Enumerated Types

Enumerated types declare an alternate type name and an array of identifiers. You may use these identifiers as values for the data type you are working with. All enumerators are constants whose data type is the given enumeration.

To generate an enumeration, you should use **enum** (a C++ keyword). Here is the syntax that you should use:

```
enum enum-name { list of names } var-list;
```

In this syntax, "enum-name" represents the type name of the enumeration. You should use commas to separate the names inside the brackets.

For instance, the code given below creates an enumeration called sizes, gives it three different sizes, and a variable (i.e. c) to determine the type size. Lastly, "large" is assigned to the c-variable.

enum sizes { small, medium, large } c;

c = large;

By default, the first name's value is equal to 0, the second name's value is equal to 1, the third name's value is equal to 2, etc. However, you can add an initializer to assign a certain value to your selected names.

For instance, in the enumeration given below, **medium** will get the value 100.

enum sizes { small, medium=100, large };

A name's value is 1 greater than the one before it. Thus, in the latest example, the value of large is equal to 101.

Variable Types

Variables provide you with storage that can be modified and controlled by your programs. Every variable belongs to a certain type, which states the following:

- The layout and size of the memory space

- The values that you can store inside the memory space

- The operations that you can apply

You may use the underscore, numbers and letters when naming a variable. However, you can't use a number as the first character of the variable's name. For example, variable1 is valid but 1variable isn't. Additionally, this programming language is case-sensitive. That means VARIABLE, Variable, and variable are considered as three different entities.

At this point, let's describe the different variable types discussed in the previous chapter:

Variable Type	Description
int	This is the natural integer size for programming.
bool	This variable can store true or false values.
void	It represents the lack of variable type.
char	This is one of the integer types. Often, it is represented as a single byte (i.e. one octet).
float	This variable type is a single precision floating point value.
wchar_t	It represents wide characters.
double	This variable type is a double precision floating point value.

Additionally, the C++ programming language allows you to define other variable types using methods and certain tools (e.g. classes, array, data structures, etc.).

The next part of the book will explain how you can describe, declare, and utilize different variable types.

How to Define Variables in C++

By defining a variable, you are informing the C++ compiler regarding the location and storage space you want to use for the variable involved. Your variable definitions specify the data type, and hold a list of the variables that belong to that type. Here's the syntax:

type variable_list;

In this syntax, **type** should be a C++-compatible data type (e.g. int, bool, float, etc.). The **variable_list**, on the other hand, might hold single or multiple identifier names. If you have more than one identifier, separate the entries using commas. Here are some legitimate variable declarations:

int a, z, x;

double y;

char x, a;

float z, extra;

The section **int a, z, x;** both defines and declares the variables a, z, and k; this tells the C++ compiler to generate variables named a, z, and k that belongs to the int type.

You may initialize (i.e. assign a value to a variable) your variables during the declaration phase. The initializers in C++ have two main parts: (1) an equal sign, and (2) a constant expression. Here's the syntax:

```
type variable_name = value;
```

Here are some valid initializers:

int x = 4, z = 10;   // definition and initialization of x and z.

byte a = 99;   // definition and initialization of a.

char b = 'b';   // the variable named b has the value 'b'.

How to Declare Variables in C++

Variable declarations assure the C++ compiler that a variable exists with the specified name and type. That means the language compiler can complete the compilation process without having to perform further analysis regarding the variable. Variable declarations have their meaning during the compile-time only. C++ compilers require actual variable declarations while the program is being linked.

You'll find variable declarations extremely useful when you have several available files and you specify a variable in one of them. You should use **extern**, another C++ keyword, when declaring a variable in your statements. This language allows you to declare the same variable several times in your program. However, you can only define it once in a function, file, or code block.

Rvalues and Lvalues

The C++ language supports two types of expressions:

- rvalue – This term refers to a value stored somewhere in the memory. Rvalues are expressions that cannot hold the value/s assigned to them. That means you may place an rvalue on the right-hand side, but never on the left-hand side, of your C++ statements.

- lvalue – These are expressions that point to a specific memory location. You can place lvalues on either side of your C++ statements.

All variables are classified as lvalues. That means they can appear on the right-hand and left-hand side of your statements. Numeric literals, on the other hand, are considered as rvalues. That means they cannot be written on the left-side of a C++ statement.

CHAPTER 5

The Scope of a Variable

Basically, the term "scope" refers to a part of a C++ program. Here are three areas where you can declare variables:

- Outside the functions of your program. These variables are known as global variables since they can be accessed at any part of the program.

- Inside a block or function. Variables declared this way are known as local variables.

- Inside the definition of a function parameter. These parameters are known as formal parameters.

In this section of the book, you'll learn about the global and local variables. Formal parameters will be discussed in a later chapter.

The Global Variables

These variables are declared outside the functions. Typically, global variables are placed on the top section of C++ programs. Variables that belong to this type can store their value permanently.

You may access global variables using any function; thus, you may utilize global variables at any part of your program.

The Local Variables

These variables are declared within a block or function. Since these variables are placed within a certain function or code block, you can only use them for statements that are located in the same function or block. You cannot use local variables for external statements (i.e. statements stored outside the function or block of code).

How to Initialize Global and Local Variables

Once local variables are defined, the system won't initialize them. That means you have to initialize them manually. On the other hand, the system initializes global variables automatically. Here are some valid data types and their corresponding initializer:

Data Type	The Initializer
char	'\0'
int	o
float	0
pointer	NULL
double	0

Important Note: While writing programs, you should initialize all of your variables properly. If you won't, your programs might generate unexpected or unwanted results.

CHAPTER 6

Literals/Constants

The term "constant" refers to a fixed value that can prevent your program from making future alterations. This kind of value is also known as a literal.

Important Note: C++ programs treat literals as ordinary variables. The only difference is that programs cannot modify these literals in any way.

Literals can belong to any of the fundamental data types. Expert programmers divide these values into five major categories. These are:

Boolean Values

The C++ programming language has two Boolean constants, which are considered as keywords:

- false – A value that represents false.

- true – A value that represents true.

Important Note: True is not equal to 1 and false is not equal to 0.

Characters

You should enclose character constants using single quotes. Constants that begin with L (uppercase) belong to the "wide character" category and must be stored inside a **wchar_t** variable. If your constant doesn't begin with an uppercase L, on the other hand, it is considered as a narrow character and can be kept inside a simple **char** variable.

Character constants can take the form of plain characters (e.g. 'y'), universal characters (e.g. '\u01C0'), or escape sequences (e.g. '\n').

In the C++ programming language, some characters gain a special function if they are introduced by a backslash. These characters are known as sequence codes. Check the following examples:

The Escape Sequence	The Meaning
\'	Single quote
\?	Question mark
\"	Double quote
\\	Backslash
\b	Backspace
\f	Form feed
\a	Bell or alert
\n	Newline
\000	An octal number that has 1 – 3 digits
\v	Vertical tab
\r	Carriage return
\xhh	Hexadecimal number
\t	Horizontal tab

Strings

You must enclose string constants using double quotes. Strings contain characters similar to that of character constants: escape sequences, universal characters, and plain characters.

String constants allow you to divide long lines into smaller ones. If you'll use this functionality, you should add whitespaces between the smaller lines to separate them.

Floating-Point

Floating-point constants have four parts: (1) exponent, (2) fraction, (3) integer, and (4) decimal point. You may represent these constants either in exponential or decimal form.

When writing a floating-point literal in the decimal form, include the exponent, the decimal point, or both. When writing in the exponential form, on the other hand, you should include the fraction, the integer, or both. Introduce signed exponents using an E or e.

Integers

Integer constants can be octal, decimal, or hexadecimal literals. You should use a prefix to specify the radix (i.e. the base of the value) of these constants. Here are the integer constants and their corresponding prefix:

- Decimal Integers – nothing

- Octal Integers – o

- Hexadecimal Integers – oX

The C++ language allows you to add L and/or U (L stands for long, U stands for unsigned) as suffix for your integer literals. These suffixes are not case-sensitive. Also, you can place them in any order.

The list below will show you some integer constants:

- 0xFalL   // Valid

- 616   // Valid

- 615U   // Valid

- 049   // Invalid - 9 is not an octal number

- 065   // Invalid – You cannot repeat any suffix

Here are some samples of valid Integer constants:

- 65   // decimal
- 0312   // octal
- 20   // int
- 20u   // unsigned int
- 20ul   // unsigned long
- 20l   // long

How to Define a Constant

In this programming language, you can define literals in two different ways:

- using const (a C++ keyword)
- using #define (a C++ preprocessor)

What is **#define**?

This preprocessor uses the following syntax while defining literals:

```
#define identifier value
```

The example below will help you understand this preprocessor:

```
#include <iostream>
using namespace std;

#define LENGTH 10
#define WIDTH  5
#define NEWLINE '\n'
#include <iostream>
using namespace std;

#define LENGTH 10
#define WIDTH  5
#define NEWLINE '\n'
```

If you will compile and execute the code given above, you'll get this result: **50**.

What is **const**?

Basically, const is a C++ keyword that you can use to declare literals with a particular type. Here is the syntax of this keyword:

```
const type variable = value;
```

Important Note: According to expert programmers, you should use capital letters when defining literals.

CHAPTER 7

Modifiers and Storage Classes

The Different Kinds of Modifiers in the C++ Language

In the C++ language, you may use modifiers to introduce **double**, **int**, and **char** data types. Modifiers allow you to change the meaning of data types so that they can meet your needs.

This section will discuss the following modifiers:

- short

- long

- unsigned

- signed

You may apply all of these modifiers when working on integer constants. Additionally, you can apply **unsigned** and **signed** on **char** constants. Finally, you can apply **long** on double-precision floating point literals.

Important Note: This programming language allows you to combine modifiers. You may use **signed** and **unsigned** to introduce **short** or **long** modifiers. For instance, **signed short int**.

C++ offers a shortcut for declaring long, short, or unsigned integers. You may simply enter long, short, or unsigned, respectively. This programming language will add int automatically. For instance, the two statements given below both declare short integer variables:

short a;

short int z;

The following screenshot shows the code of a simple program. This program will help you understand how C++ interprets signed and unsigned modifiers.

```cpp
#include <iostream>
using namespace std;


/* This program shows the difference between
 * signed and unsigned integers.
 */
int main()
{
    short int i;              // a signed short integer
    short unsigned int j;   // an unsigned short integer

    j = 50000;


    i = j;
    cout << i << " " << << j;


    return 0;
}
```

If you have entered and run the program correctly, you'll get the following result:

```
-15536 50000
```

The Different Kinds of Qualifiers

A type qualifier provides useful data about the variable it precedes. Here are the qualifiers that you will encounter while using C++:

Name of Qualifier	The Meaning
volatile	This modifier informs the C++ compiler that the value of a variable can be changed using methods that are not specified in the statement.
restrict	This modifier provides you with different access methods to an object.
const	You can use this modifier to prevent your program from changing an object during the execution phase.

The Storage Classes in C++

Storage classes define the visibility (also known as scope) and lifetime of functions and/or variables inside a program. A storage class is a modifier that precedes the object type that it modifies. The C++ language supports five storage classes, namely:

- static

- auto

- extern

- mutable

- register

Let's discuss each storage class in detail:

Static

This storage class tells the C++ compiler to keep a local variable as long as a program is active. This is because C++ programs sometimes create and destroy variables on a continuous cycle. Thus, tagging local variables as static allows those variables to retain their values even if they go in/out of scope.

You may also apply this modifier on global variables. Once you have applied this modifier, the scope of the variable will be limited to the file it is declared in.

Auto

This serves as the default class for defining local variables. Here's a basic example:

```
{
    int mount;
    auto int month;
}
```

This sample code defines two different variables that belong to the same class. You can only use **auto** inside functions. That means you can only apply this storage class on local variables.

Extern

With this storage class, you can make references to global variables that are accessible to all of your program files. When using this extern, you cannot initialize the variable since it only points the variable name to a memory location you have defined previously.

If you have several files and you have defined a global function or variable, which can also be used in different files, you may use extern on a different file to reference your predefined function or variable.

This modifier is typically used when the programmer has multiple files that share similar global functions or variables.

Mutable

You can only apply this modifier on class objects. The **mutable** storage class allows an object's member to override the **const** function.

Register

You should use this storage class when defining local variables that must be saved inside a register (i.e. not in the machine's RAM). Thus, the variable's maximum size is equal to the register's size (typically a single word). Additionally, these variables cannot possess the "&" operator since they don't have a specific location in the computer's memory.

In general, you should use this register to store variables that need fast access (e.g. counters). It is important to note that defining a "register" is different from storing a variable in the register. That means you can store quick-access variables inside a register, based on implementation and hardware limitations.

CHAPTER 8

The Operators in the C++ Language

In this programming language, operators are symbols that require the compiler to conduct logical or mathematical manipulations. The C++ language offers a wide range of pre-installed operators. These are:

The Logical Operators

The list below will show you the logical operators available in the C++ programming language. Let's assume that x = 2 and y = 0.

- "||" – This operator is known as "Logical OR." The condition is true if one of the operands is not equal to zero. For instance: (x || y) is true.

- "&&" – This is called "Logical AND." If the two operands are not equal to zero, the condition is true. Here's an example: (x && y) is false.

- "!" – Programmers call this operator "logical NOT." You can use it to reverse the status of an operand. If the condition is false, "!" will give you true. For example: !(x && y) is true.

The Arithmetic Operators

In this part of the book, you'll learn about the arithmetic operators available in C++. To help you understand how each operator works, let's use two sample variables: x = 1; y = 3.

- "+" – This operator adds operands. For example: x + y = 4.

- "-" – You should use this operator to perform subtraction. It subtracts the value of the right-hand operand from that of the left-hand operand. For instance: $y - x = 2$.

- "*" – This operator allows you to perform multiplication on your C++ statements. For instance: $x * y = 3$.

- "/" – With this operator, you can conduct division on your C++ codes. For example: $y / x = 3$.

- "++" – This is known as the increment operator. It increases the value of an operand by one. For example: $y++ = 4$.

- "—" – This is called the decrement operator. With this, you can decrease the operand's value by one. For instance: $x-- = 0$.

The Assignment Operators

Here, you'll learn about the assignment operators offered by C++:

- "=" – This operator is called "simple assignment." It assigns the value/s of the right-hand operand to the left-hand operand. For instance: $(z = x + y)$ assigns the value of $x + y$ to z.

- "+=" This is known as "Add AND." It adds the values of both operands and assigns the sum to the left-hand operand. For example: $(z += x)$ is equal to $(z = z + x)$.

- "*=" – Programmers call this the "Multiply AND" operator. It multiplies the value of the left-hand operand with that of the right-hand operand and gives the result to the left-hand operand. For example: $(z *= x)$ is equal to $(z = z * x)$.

- "-=" – This operator is called "Subtract AND." It subtracts the value of the right-hand operand from that of the left-hand operand and assigns the difference to the left-hand operand. For instance: $(z -= x)$ is equal to $(z = z - x)$.

- "/=" This is called the "Divide AND" operator. It dives the value of the left-hand operand with that of the right-hand operand and assigns the quotient to the left-hand operand. For example: (z /= x) is equal to (z = z / x).

- "&=" – This is called the "Bitwise AND" operator. The following example will show you how it works: (z &= x) is identical to (z = z & x).

- "|=" – Programmers refer this operator as "Bitwise inclusive OR and." Here's how it works: (z |= x) is identical to (z = z | x).

- "^=" – This is called "Bitwise exclusive OR and." It works this way: (z ^= x) is identical to (z = z ^ x).

- ">>=" – This is known as "Right shift AND." Here's how it works: (z >>= x) is identical to (z = z >> x).

- "<<=" – Programmers call this "Left shift AND." It works this way: (z <<= x) is identical to (z = z << x).

The Bitwise Operators

You can apply bitwise operators on bits. In general, you must use them to conduct bit-by-bit operations. The screenshot below shows the truth tables for &, |, and ^.

p	q	p & q	p | q	p ^ q
0	0	0	0	0
0	1	0	1	1
1	1	1	1	0
1	0	0	1	1

Let's assume that x = 60; and y = 13. If we will convert these values into their binary form, we'll get the following data:

x = 0011 1100

y = 0000 1101

x|y = 0011 1101

~x = 1100 0011

x&y = 0000 1100

x^y = 0011 0001

The table below will show you the bitwise operators available in C++. Let's assume that x = 60 and y = 13.

- "&" – This operator is known as "Binary AND." If a bit exists in the two operands, Binary AND will copy it to the result. For example: (x & y) produces 12 (i.e. 0000 1100).

- "^" – This is called the "Binary XOR." It will copy a bit if it exists in one of the operands but not both. (x ^ y) gives 49, or 0011 0001.

- "|" – Programmers refer this as the "Binary OR" operator. It will copy a bit that exists in one of the operands. For example: (x | y) will give you 61, i.e. 0011 1101.

- ">>" – This operator is known as "Binary Right Shift." It moves the value of the left-hand operand based on the bits given by the right-hand operand. For example: x >> 2 gives 15, i.e. 0000 1111.

- "<<" – This is called "Binary Left Shift." It moves the left-hand operand's value according to the number or bits given by the right-hand operand. For instance: x << 2 gives 240, i.e. 1111 0000.

- "~" – Programmers call this the "Binary Ones Complement." This is a unary operator. Additionally, it "flips" the bits it is applied to. For example: (~x) gives – 61, i.e. 1100 0011 if written in the 2's complement format because of a signed number.

The Relational Operators

This section of the book will focus on the relational operators available in the C++ programming language. Let's assume that x = 2 and y = 4.

- "==" – This operator checks the equality of two operands. If the operands are equal, the condition is true. For instance: (x == y) is not true.

- ">" – This operator checks the value of two operands. If the left-hand operand's value is greater than that of the right-hand one, the condition is true. For example: (y > x) is true.

- "<" – This operator is the opposite of "<". If the value of the left-hand operand is lesser than that of the right-hand operand, the condition is true. For instance: (y < x) is not true.

- "!=" This operator checks the equality between two operands. If the values are unequal, the condition is true. For example: (x != y) is true.

- "<=" – With this operator, you'll check whether the left-hand operand's value is less than or equal to that of the right-hand operand. If it is, the condition is true. For example: (x <= y) is true.

- ">=" – Here, you'll check if the left-hand operand's value is greater than or equal to that of the right-hand operand. If it is, the condition is true. For instance: (y >= x) is true.

The Miscellaneous Operators

In this section, you'll learn about other operators offered by C++:

- "sizeof" - You should use this operator to determine a variable's size. For instance, sizeof(x), where x is an integer, will give you 4.

- "Cast" – This operator allows you to convert data types.

- "," – Programmers refer to this as the "comma operator." It activates a group of operations in your statements. The comma expression's value is equal to that of the last item in the comma-separated set.

- "." and "->" – These operators are known as "dot" and "arrow," respectively. You can use these operators to reference the members of unions, classes, and structures.

- "*" – This is known as the "pointer" variable. For instance: *new; will generate a pointer to a variable named new.

- "&" – This operator can give you the address of any variable. For instance, &x; will provide you with the address of that variable.

- "Condition ? X : Y" – This is known as the conditional operator. If the condition is true, this operator will give you the value of x. If it false, however, the operator will give you the value of y.

The Operator Precedence in the C++ Language

Operator precedence dictates the division of terms in C++ expressions. This precedence influences how the system evaluates expressions. Some operators are lower than others in terms of precedence. For instance, the subtraction operator (i.e. "-") has lower precedence than the division operator (i.e. "/").

Here's a simple mathematical expression: (x = 8 – 6 /2). In this expression, x's value is 5, not 1 since "-" has lower precedence than "/" (i.e. subtraction will be performed after division). Thus, 6 will be divided by 2. Then, the quotient will be subtracted from 8.

CHAPTER 9

The Different Types of Loops in C++

In some cases, you might need to repeat blocks of code several times. Typically, C++ statements are conducted in a sequential manner: the system executes statements according to their position in the code.

The C++ programming language offers different structures for controlling blocks of codes. With these structures, you can easily manipulate codes even if they have complex execution paths.

Loop statements allow you to execute one statement or a set of statements several times. The screenshot given below shows the basic form of loop statements in major computer languages:

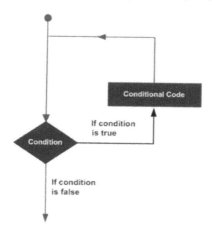

C++ offers the following loop types:

Type of Loop	Definition
for loop	This loop type executes a group of statements several times. It also shortens the code that controls the looping variable.
while loop	This type will repeat statements as long as a specified condition is met. Basically, while loop checks the condition prior to performing the body of the loop.
do… while loop	This is similar to a while loop. The only difference is that a "do… while loop" checks the condition once the loop body has been executed.
nested loop	You may place a loop or a set of loops within an existing "for," "while," or "do… while" loop.

Let's discuss each loop type in detail:

The While Loop

This loop type executes the targeted statement repeatedly while the specified condition is true.

The Syntax

Here is the syntax of a C++ while loop:

```
while(condition)
{
    statement(s);
}
```

In this syntax, statement(s) can be an individual statement or a group of statements. On the other hand, (condition) can take the form of any C++ expression, and true must be a non-zero value. Keep in mind that this loop will repeat the selected statement as long as the condition is true.

If the condition is false, the system passes program control to the line after the while loop.

The Diagram of a While Loop

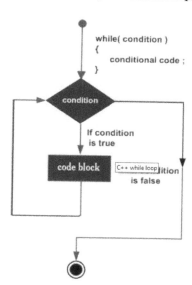

Based on this diagram, it is possible that a while loop will never run. If the condition is false, the system will ignore the loop's body and execute the statements after the loop.

The For Loop

This loop is a control structure that helps you to write loops efficiently. This loop type is particularly useful when you have to execute loops multiple times.

The syntax for this loop type is:

```
for ( init; condition; increment )
{
    statement(s);
}
```

The following list explains the control flow of "for loops:"

1. **init** – The system executes this step first (and once only). You can use this part to create and activate variables for loop control. This part isn't mandatory – placing a semicolon is enough if you don't have any entry for **init**.

2. **condition** – In this part of the syntax, you must specify the condition you want to use. If the result of the condition is true, the loop's body will be executed. If the result is false, however, the loop's body will be ignored. Then, the system will pass the control flow to the statement after the loop.

3. **increment** – You can use this part to modify the variables for loop control. You may simply place a semicolon on this part – it is not mandatory. Basically, **increment** becomes useful once the loop body is performed.

4. The system will recheck the condition's result. If the result is true, the loop statement activates and the procedure starts again. This loop will terminate once the result becomes false.

The Flow Diagram of a For Loop

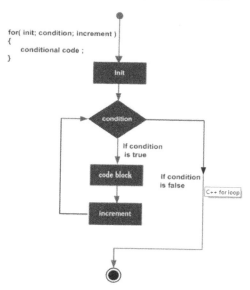

The Do... While Loop

Unlike the previous loop types, which check the condition before executing the loop's body, "do... while" checks the specified condition once the loop has been performed.

Do... while loops are similar to while loops, the only difference is that do... while loops will execute at least once (regardless of the condition's result).

The syntax of C++ "do... while" loops is:

```
do
{
    statement(s);
}while( condition );
```

As you can see, the condition is given at the loop's final section. That means the loop will execute prior to testing the specified condition.

If the result is true, the control flow will be restarted and the targeted statement will be repeated again. This procedure will be repeated until the condition's result becomes false.

The Flow Diagram of Do... While Loops

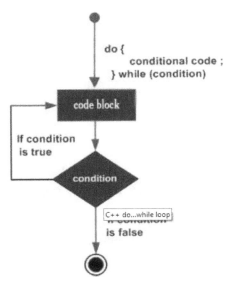

The Nested Loops

C++ allows you to place loops inside another loop. This process is called "nesting" a loop. The syntax for this type depends on the loop you want to nest:

The Syntax for Nested For Loops

```
for ( init; condition; increment )
{
    for ( init; condition; increment )
    {
        statement(s);
    }
    statement(s); // you can put more statements.
}
```

The Syntax for Nested While Loops

```
while(condition)
{
    while(condition)
    {
        statement(s);
    }
    statement(s); // you can put more statements.
}
```

The Syntax for Do... While Loops

```
do
{
    statement(s); // you can put more statements.
    do
    {
        statement(s);
    }while( condition );

}while( condition );
```

What is a Loop Control Statement?

A loop control statement can alter the execution of a loop's body. Once the execution is altered, all of the automatic objects you created for the previous process will be destroyed.

The C++ programming language supports these loop control statements:

The Control Statement	Definition
goto statement	This statement can transfer the loop control to a targeted statement. You should not use this loop control statement in your C++ programs.
continue statement	This statement can cause the loop to ignore the rest of its body and check the condition immediately before reiteration.
break statement	Break statements can terminate the switch or loop statement and pass control to the C++ statement after the switch or loop.

Let's discuss each loop control statement in detail:

The "goto" Statement

Basically, goto statements allow you to set unconditional jumps in your functions.

Important Note: Often, it is extremely hard to trace the flow of program control when goto statements are being used. That means you might encounter problems in reading or modifying your C++ programs if you'll use a goto statement. Because of this reason, you are advised to stay away from this loop control statement.

Here is the syntax of a C++ goto statement:

```
goto label;
..
.
label: statement;
```

In the syntax given above, **label** is the identifier that specifies your labeled statement/s. Here is the syntax of C++ goto statements:

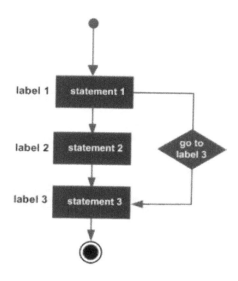

The "continue" Statement

Continue statements force the activation of a loop. They also ignore codes that may affect the loop's functions.

When it comes to **for** loops, this forced continuation executes the loop's conditional check and increment parts. For while and do... while loops, however, control of the program is passed on to the conditional check.

The syntax of C++ "continue" statements is:

continue;

Here is the flow diagram of continue statements:

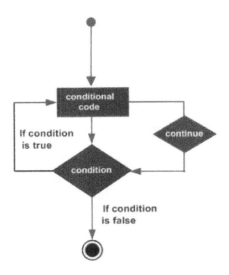

The "break" Statement

This statement serves two purposes in the C++ language:

- If the system encounters a break statement within a loop, that loop will be terminated. Then, program control will be passed on to the statement after the loop.

- You can use it to end a case in your switch statement (you'll learn about it in the next chapter).

For nested loops, break statements will terminate the innermost loop and execute the line after the code block.

Here is the syntax of a C++ break statement:

break;

The Flow Diagram of a Break Statement

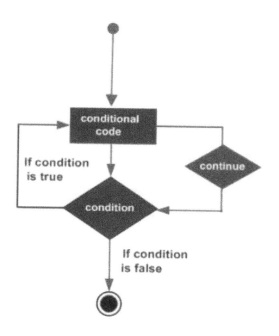

Infinite Loops

Loops become infinite if their condition is always true. In general, programmers use **for** loops to achieve this goal. Since the expressions involved in a "for" loop are optional, you can create endless loops just by leaving the condition part empty. Here's an example:

```
#include <iostream>
using namespace std;

int main ()
{

    for( ; ; )
    {
        printf("This loop will run forever.\n");
    }

    return 0;
}
```

Conditional expressions are supposed to be true if they aren't present. C++ users usually employ 'for (;;)' to represent infinite loops. However, you may include an increment and initialization expression in your C++ statements.

Important Note: You can press Ctrl + C to terminate infinite loops.

CHAPTER 10

The Decision-Making Statements in C++

A decision making structure requires you to indicate conditions, which can be tested or evaluated by your C++ program. You should also provide statements that will be run based on the condition's result (i.e. either true or false). The image below shows the basic structure of a normal decision-making statement in C++ programs:

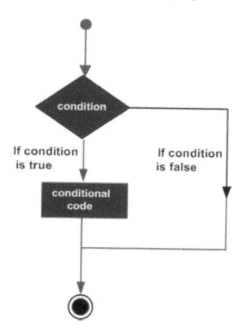

The C++ language offers the following decision-making statements:

Name of Statement	Definition
switch statement	This kind of statement allows you to test a variable's equality against a group of values.
if statement	Generally, an "if" statement involves a Boolean expression and one or more C++ statements.
if... else statement	C++ allows you to place an "else" statement after an "if" statement. The "else" statement will run if the specified Boolean condition is false.
nested switch statement	You may place a "switch" statement inside an existing "switch" statement.
nested	You may place an "if" or "if else" statement inside an "if" or "if else" statement.

Let's discuss each decision-making statement in detail:

Switch Statements

Switch statements allow you to check a variable's equality against a set of values. These values are called cases – the variable you want to check will be compared with each case.

The syntax of C++ switch statements is:

```
switch(expression){
    case constant-expression  :
        statement(s);
        break; //optional
    case constant-expression  :
        statement(s);
        break; //optional


    // you can have any number of case statements.
    default : //Optional
        statement(s);
}
```

When working with a switch statement, there are certain rules that you need to remember. These rules are:

- The **expression** of your switch statement should be an enumerated or integral class type. Alternatively, it may belong to a type where classes have one conversion function to the enumerated or integral class types.

- C++ doesn't have a limit regarding the amount of case statements that you can add into your **switch**. However, make sure that each case has a colon and a value you can compare to.

- The case's constant-expression and switch's variable must belong to the same type of data. Additionally, your constant-expression must be a literal.

- If the variable you're switching on is equivalent to one of the cases, the statements after that case will run until the system reaches a break statement.

- Once the system reaches a break statement, the switch statement will stop. Then, the control flow will be passed on to the line after the switch.

- You don't have to place a break statement in all of your cases. If a case doesn't have break, the control flow will be passed on to the next cases until the system finds a break statement.

- You may add a default case to your switch statements. In C++, you should include the default case at the end of your statement. Programmers generally use default cases when they need to perform a task but all of the cases are false. Additionally, default cases don't need break statements.

The Flow Diagram of a Switch Statement

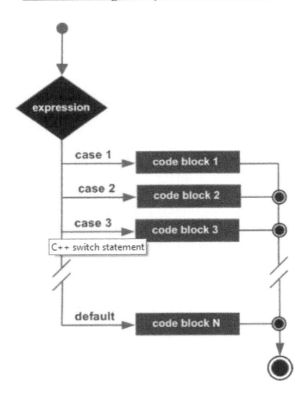

If Statements

Basically, an "if" statement involves one Boolean expression and a statement or a group of statements.

Here is the syntax of a C++ if statement:

```
if(boolean_expression)
{
    // statement(s) will execute if the boolean expression is true
}
```

If the result of the Boolean expression is true, the system will execute the code block within the "if" statement. If the result is false, however, the system will execute the code found after the "if" statement.

The flow diagram of an "if" statement is:

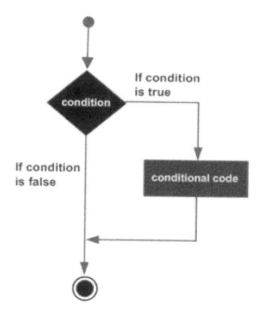

If Else Statements

You may include an "else" statement after the "if" statement. This optional "else" statement runs if the result of the Boolean expression is false.

The syntax of this statement is:

```
if(boolean_expression)
{
    // statement(s) will execute if the boolean expression is true
}
else
{
    // statement(s) will execute if the boolean expression is false
}
```

The code's "if" section will run if the expression Boolean expression's result is true. If the result is false, on the other hand, the "else" section of the code will run instead.

The Flow Diagram of an "If Else" Statement

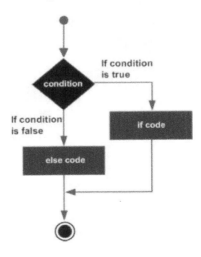

Nested Switch Statements

C++ allows you to use a switch as a part of another switch. You won't encounter any problems even if the constants of the outer and inner switch hold identical values.

In this programming language, you may use about 256 nesting levels for your switch statements.

Here is the syntax for a C++ nested switch:

```
switch(ch1) {
   case 'A':
       cout << "This A is part of outer switch";
       switch(ch2) {
          case 'A':
              cout << "This A is part of inner switch";
              break;
          case 'B': // ...
       }
       break;
   case 'B': // ...
}
```

Nested If Statements

You can always nest an "if else" statement in your codes. That means you may add an "if" or "if else" statement inside a different "if" or "if else" statement.

Here is the syntax of this C++ statement:

```
if( boolean_expression 1)
{
    // Executes when the boolean expression 1 is true
    if(boolean_expression 2)
    {
        // Executes when the boolean expression 2 is true
    }
}
```

CHAPTER 11

The Different Functions in C++

Functions are group of statements designed to perform a particular task. Each program written using C++ has a function, which exists in the **main()** section of the code. Additionally, even the simplest C++ programs can have extra functions.

C++ allows you to divide your code into different functions. The method of division depends on your needs and preferences, although you have to make sure that each function accomplishes a certain task.

Function **declarations** inform the C++ compiler regarding the name, parameters, and return type of a function. Function **definitions**, on the other hand, give the function's actual body.

The standard library of this programming language offers different functions. Here are two basic functions and their capabilities:

- strcat() – This function concatenates two strings.

- memcpy() – It copies a memory location to a different one.

Important Note: Some programmers refer to functions as methods, procedures, or sub-routines.

How to Define a Function

Here is the syntax of functions in C++:

```
return_type function_name( parameter list )
{
    body of the function
}
```

Let's discuss the different parts of a C++ function:

- Name – This is the function's actual name.

- Parameters – Programmers consider parameters as placeholders. Whenever you invoke a function, you give a value to the function's parameter. C++ users refer to this value as an argument or actual parameter. The list of parameters refers to the order, number, and type of the function's parameters. Keep in mind that parameters aren't mandatory: your functions can be active even without any parameter.

- Return Type – Functions can retrieve a value. The values returned by a function belong to a data type called "**return_type**." In some cases, functions perform the required task without retrieving any value. Here, the **return_type** of the data is "**void**."

- Function Body – This part holds a group of C++ statements that determine the purpose and capabilities of the function.

How to Declare a Function

Function declarations inform the C++ compiler about functions (i.e. their name and how to call them). You may define the function's body separately.

Function declarations have these parts:

```
return_type function_name( parameter list );
```

You don't have to worry about parameter names while declaring a function. You can simply focus on the function's type. That means the declaration below is valid:

```
int max(int, int);
```

You have to use a function declaration if you'll call a function that is defined in another source file. In this situation, you must declare the needed function on top of the source file requiring the function.

How to Call a Function

When you create a function in C++, you define the function's purpose. To run a function, you should invoke or call the function.

When C++ programs run a function, the system transfers the program control to the invoked function. An invoked function conducts the assigned task. Once it completely executes its return statement or reaches its closing brace, the system returns the program control to the C++ program.

To invoke a function, you just have to specify the function's name and pass the parameters. You may store any value that will be returned by the function.

The Arguments of a C++ Function

If your function has arguments, you should declare variables that are compatible with the arguments' values. Programmers refer to these variables as "formal parameters."

Generally, formal parameters act like ordinary variables located within the function. They pop into existence once the program enters the function. Then, they disappear as soon as the program exits the function.

When you call a function, you can pass arguments to the function in three different ways. These are:

Type of Call	Definition
By pointer	This technique sends the argument's address into the formal parameter/s. Basically, the address helps you to access the argument involved in the call. Thus, the modifications on the parameter influence the argument.
By value	In this technique, the argument's actual value is sent to the function's formal parameter. In this situation, modifications on the parameter within the function don't influence the argument.
By reference	This technique copies the argument's reference and gives it to the function's formal parameter. Within the function, references help you to access the arguments involved in the call. Thus, the changes applied on the parameter influence the argument.

Following is more information regarding each technique:

By Pointer

To forward values using this technique, you should pass argument pointers to the function as if you are working with ordinary values. That means you must declare each parameter as a pointer type.

By Value

This technique copies the real value of the argument and gives it to the function's formal parameter. Actually, this technique serves as the default method of passing arguments in the C++ programming language.

Important Note: Codes located inside a function cannot change the arguments involved in invoking that function.

By Reference

To pass values using this technique, you just have to think that you are working on ordinary values. Declare the parameter/s of the function as the reference type/s.

The Default Values of Parameters in C++

While defining a function, you may assign a default value to the last parameter. You'll benefit from this default value once you encounter a blank argument while invoking a function.

You can assign a default value through an assignment operator. Then, place values for the correct arguments in the function's definition. If the system doesn't get any value when the function is invoked, it will use the default value you assigned. If a value is returned, however, the default value will be ignored.

CHAPTER 12

Numbers in the C++ Language

When working with numbers, you typically use basic types of data (e.g. int, long, short, double, float, etc.). You have learned about these data types in an earlier chapter.

How to Perform Mathematical Operations in the C++ Language

Aside from the different functions that you may create, C++ offers powerful pre-installed functions. You can access these functions through the libraries of C and C++ languages. C++ allows you to include these functions in your programs.

The C++ programming language provides an excellent collection of math operations, which you can perform on different numbers.

The table below shows some of the most useful mathematical operations offered by C++:

Mathematical Function	Purpose
double tan(double);	With this function, you can get the tangent of an angle by taking it as a double.
double cos(double);	It allows you to get the cosine by taking any angle as a double.
double log(double);	By using this function, you can determine a number's natural log.
double sin(double);	This function allows you to get the sine of an angle.

Mathematical Function	Purpose
double sqrt(double);	You can get the square root of any number by passing it into this function.
double pow(double, double);	This function has two elements: (1) the number you want to raise, and (2) the power you want to raise the number to.
int abs(int);	With this function, you can get an integer's absolute value.
double hypot(double, double);	This function allows you to get the length of a right triangle's hypotenuse. However, you must provide the length of the remaining sides.
double floor(double);	This function searches for an integer that is lesser than or equal to the assigned argument.
double fabs(double);	With this function, you can get a decimal number's absolute value.

CHAPTER 13

C++ Arrays

This programming language offers the "array," which is a data structure. Arrays keep a sequential set of elements that belong to the same type. Programmers use arrays to store groups of data, although it is more beneficial to consider arrays as sets of variables that belong to the same type.

Rather than declaring variables one by one (e.g. number1, number2, number3, etc.), you may declare an array variable (e.g. number) and represent the variables using number[1], number[2], number[3], etc. You can access elements inside an array using an index.

Each array has adjacent memory locations. The lowest memory location links to the first object in the array while the highest memory location links to the final object.

How to Declare an Array

When declaring an array, you should specify the type and quantity of the elements needed in the array. Here's the syntax that you should use:

```
type arrayName [ arraySize ];
```

This array is known as "single-dimension." Your array's "arraySize" section should hold an integer literal that is greater than zero. The "type" section, on the other hand, should contain any data type supported by C++. For instance, you should use the statement below to declare an array that holds 10 elements. This array is named balance and the data type is **double**.

```
double balance[10];
```

How to Initialize an Array

In the C++ language, you may initialize array elements in two ways: (1) individually, or (2) through a single C++ statement (see the example below).

```
double balance[5] = {1000.0, 2.0, 3.4, 17.0, 50.0};
```

The values between the curly braces must always be lower than or equal to the quantity of elements you declared inside the brackets.

How to Access an Array Element

You can access array elements by indexing the name of the array. To do this, enter the element's index number inside the brackets after the array's name.

The Different C++ Concepts Related to Arrays

Arrays play a huge part in using C++ for writing programs. Thus, you should be familiar with them. The list below shows the most important array-related concepts in the C++ language. As a C++ user, you have to master the following concepts:

Concept	Explanation
Pointers to existing arrays	C++ allows you to create a pointer to the array's initial element just by entering the array's name. Here, you don't have to include any index.

Concept	Explanation
Multi-dimensional array	This programming language allows you to create multi-dimensional arrays. Obviously, two-dimensional arrays are the most basic multi-dimensional arrays you can create.
Passing an array to a function	You may pass an array's pointer to a function. To do this, you just have to specify the name of the array. You should not enter any index.
Getting an array from a function	In C++, you can retrieve arrays from a function.

Conclusion

I hope this book was able to help you learn the basics of C++.

The next step is to use C++ in writing your own computer programs.

Would you do me a favor?

Finally, if you enjoyed this book, please take the time to share your thoughts and post a positive review on Amazon. It'd be greatly appreciated!

Thank you and good luck!

Lightning Source UK Ltd.
Milton Keynes UK
UKOW06f1847080816

280248UK00014B/295/P